Southernmost Point
Guest House

Pretend Genius Press

www.pretendgenius.com

Published simultaneously in the United States and Great Britain in 2014
by Pretend Genius Press

This compilation copyright © Pretend Genius Press 2014
Edited by Feargal Mooney

ISBN 978-0-9852133-9-8

Contents

"Take them, Love, the book and me together.
Where the heart lies, let the brain lie also."

Alex Barr

Southernmost Point Guest House

My Blue Express

Southernmost Point Guest House

The night is giving itself such airs–
heavy scents not quite incense.
Beyond the black cutout leaves and hanging roots
of a giant ficus tree, a lighted window
is sliced by the horizontals of a blind.
A cock in the distance crows
into the deep recesses of the dark.

Leaving Europe I strained against my seat-belt,
saw the grey wing with its *fault access cover*,
wanted home, the ducks driven late to bed,
the stove red in the dark, the heat of your sleeping back.
I thought of the Ten Perfections one by one.
My death sat quiet in the seat beside me
patiently, having swallowed all the ones
I dream I might have been.

Here I'm alive among a million leaves,
a hundred lights. Let them all come,
those ghosts of unriddled selves –
editor, preacher, artist, activist –
with all their thirst and clinging
like bats around this little balcony
crowding this brief scene in a different life
until at last they vanish
into the proud night that will devour them.

My Blue Express

I wish I still had the train my father made
with those blunt square hands that saved
string from parcels, punished lying, plied
a rake. That were white and puffy when he died.

After the war, when toys were hard
to find, he carved the engine like the *Mallard:*
a streamlined sloping front, fairings to hide
the cylinders curving gracefully either side

but short like a tank engine. It had no motor.
Maybe he thought that could be added later
from Basset-Lowke's wonder-catalogue. Wheels,
figures with luggage, signal gantries, rails

never arrived. There were two carriages,
cornflower blue like the engine. The edges
of the sides against the roof were imperfect
in spite of careful sanding – which I liked

because it showed exactly how they were made.
I could pull off the roofs and sides to lay
the travellers' domain bare for my inspection.
One carriage had space for a guard and parcels.

There were side corridors and compartments
just as in forties films. Facing seats
were covered in thin felt, emerald green.
He and I never talked about the train.

I admired it, rather than played with it, alone,
imagined it clacking across the Nullarbor Plain
or climbing the endless loops towards Darjeeling
(journeys I've yet to take). And did he fling

my blue train away, uncared for, when
at last he was able to buy me a clockwork one?
On my bench lie some of the tools he left me,
sunlit, the handles gleaming softly.

I wish that I could say to him that now I know
how things we make can show with each squeeze of glue,
each stroke of saw and hammer, each coat of varnish,
love we can find no other way to publish.

Andrew Mayne

Stones

Stones

Now, digging, I know these stones.
Beneath a thin soil skin they're waiting;
A spade discovers them: a thump, sparks in mud, bones shudder.
Now they must be urged, prised, woo'd.
A crowbar coaxes from the sucking mud – like pulled teeth.

My neighbour curses them; nothing grows.
"Best to keep a lawn – maybe put in a trampoline, for the kids."
But we want trees, so I must dig,
And Monaghan clay wants deep digging.

First scalp the grass;
Heave it up, trophy-like: beneath, the sunken stone skull,
The first stone's smooth skin; he crowns, awaiting a sticky birth.
The bar goes in, and with some fierce leaning, the stone may shift.
Other times, the bar strikes, sparks spit, the stone splits.
It awakes from an aeon-long snooze, shattered.

But the prised ones birth whole; ancient clay clinging.
They're smooth as babies. Once they must've called a river home.
Now my sweat wets them anew, a fresh baptism.
They pile to one side as I dig deeper.

My stones and I know what my neighbour does not know:
Beneath the rock and the clay that sucks and sticks the spade,
Another colour, not grey, but soil rust-red and fine-grained as flour.

11

Beneath that, soil black as soot:
And the roots I plant here will not retard on rock,
Nor drown in clay.

And all the stones that made way for all the trees,
I keep in a sunny corner where all might see
A quiet, flowered, rockery.

Charles Lambert

Circeo

Circeo
for Joanna

The Maga Circe lived just down the road from here
on a wooded hill overlooking the rheumatism clinic,
built under Mussolini. A low, glazed, concrete box
with a circular ramp leading down into the garden,
designed for wheelchairs, a clean, smooth sweep
from hospital bed to rose bed, from white-tiled
bathroom to the flaking blue mosaic of the fountain,
waterless this spring, perhaps because of drought.
By day, the woods are quiet. At night, but not always,
you can hear the wild boars, her enraptured suitors.
They root beneath the ruffled leaves of holm oak, bay
laurel, snuffle for acorns, truffles, the calming touch
of an orderly's hand on their bristle-haired flanks,
their earth-damp muzzles, smoothing them into sleep.
Hard to lie still beneath that spell, to wake to the body
turned into some new shape it doesn't know, outlandish
skin stretched tight on bone, blood heavy as grim death,
with nothing to do but learn one's thrall and wait
for a soothing hand, the infinite promise of release.
And it is all like a dream as you fall onto all fours.
Snout low, you sniff out the dwindling oestrogen odour
of that gilt pig through deep undergrowth, long paths
surrounded by erica, broom and myrtle, bent double,
gnarled, bright yellow flowers painful and hard as stars,
the old witch lying in her bed, all magic gone.

David Cooke

Peggy

Chez Maxe, Joinville, 1947

Peggy

My aunt Peg was a country girl
who couldn't wait to leave it.
She was flighty, flirty,
and married a gambler
with a Clark Gable moustache.

The first place they took her on
was a Camden Town tea room
where they had a Margaret,
so made her a Peggy
instead, as if that day

were a new beginning
among the fancies,
scones, and slices –
the serviettes and doilies
she insisted upon

until the end of her days –
like the fags that kept her slim,
out of sight in a wardrobe
long after, officially,
she had 'packed them in'.

In the photo they placed
on the coffin she looks
like a forties starlet. Her head
at an angle, she's staring
into a softer light

Chez Maxe, Joinville, 1947

With no finesse or finish, but still
a ladies' man, his steps are those
of a country dance or a dance
implying country matters.
No rise and fall, no pull through,
his frame dissolves in swagger
as he takes in hand his two girls
who, less impressed than he imagines,
are riding the waves of riffs and wails,
the imported sounds of freedom,
in a public space where they embrace
la vie en rose and where so recently
their sisters were stripped,
cropped, and smeared.

Geraldine Mills

Precipitation

What the Dark Becomes

Precipitation

I carry a mountain of cloud on my shoulders,
patches of fog drizzle along strands of my hair,
I open the window and rain tumbles onto my head,
thunder hangs its coat behind the door.

The weather forecaster speaks like Sylvia Plath,
tongueful of words hailstone-sharp,
clipped as the north wind that fells elms.
My mind has visibility greater than ten miles.

Indigo nimbus, cumulonimbus, violet storms
shatter the bee box under the bed,
wings, limp from damp, swarm
headlong onto the floor, buzzing.

What the Dark Becomes

Injured, the young barn owl pushed its head
into the wall trying to hollow out some darkness for itself.

Brightness blinding, its knitting needle beak clicked away
until I put it in a shoebox under the refuge of hedge.

All day it ate nothing, drank nothing
just blinked its yoke-yellow eye at me.

Listening for the slow sounding of dusk,
I carried the box to the hill, turned it on its side.

The fledging bird, dazed, flopped out, stumbled
across the grass, up, then down again.

Maybe its instinct measured the leaving of light
or wisdom to some silent homing call

because it gave a little run, a flap of wing,
flew back into the dark it swept out of me.

James Browning Kepple

the poets are calling for hangings

the poets are calling for hangings

the poets are calling for hangings
they're learning the knots,
and for not that you shall see
the noose and the trap drops,

for why then, are these of peaceful past
the holders of your oral history
laying dying in their technomuse begot,
tying porphyria with your locks

for the painters are bidding their thumbs,
languishing on tired screen shots, storage to
paint and stretch of canvas,
paint by god why not

lyres, and breathbox, player and minstrels
the songbirds are singing all that they've got,
the accordions plugging the subway vaults,
spoons from one's pocket on the hum of key

blues, dying music, a connect of bone to bellow
roar one last intake of humanimality your woes
pierce them in parakeet, slap of catgut, tonal
odes from one's maker, that we will not be made again

Judi Sutherland

It Is Written

Seattle Woman Trying to Live on Sunlight Alone
is Probably Going to Die

It Is Written

You may turn your paper over
and begin, with Gilgamesh, Utnapishtim
wedged isosceles in clay
with tax receipts and beer.
A cartouched pharaoh, smooth of glyph;
snake, and eye and ankh and falcon,
commands the desert. Wilderness
of law and prophets, writ in stone;
papyri fissured, library-deep, in jars.
Log the proud ships, passing dolphins,
sirens, sailing from Greece, bringing
mountains of gods to Rome.
Vellum scraped and cured, the Word
was God; a bug-eyed saint, a knot, a map
uncharted, *here be dragons*,
bloodied battlefields, a plough, a cross,
a pilgrim. Decrees and byelaws
scrolled, wax-sealed and ribboned;
cloistered ledgers, X marks
the signature. Lecterned folios,
leaves as fine as Bibles. A rippling flip
of turning pages. The Rose, the Globe
and all the world's a stagecoach
rattling down to Chawton.
Nibbed quill-scratching
Boswell, inkwell. The sing
of staves and clefs and quavers.
Witness of churchyard marble, overhung
with angels and blind ivy. Newsprint
hot-metalled off the presses,

chattering incessant voices,
always voices, read all about it.
Fractured orange spines of Penguins,
revolver pulp of Raymond Chandler.
Urgent business telegrams
a tickertape welcome to the dot matrix;
bit-torrent chant of laser printer;
a phosphor screen hears keyboard
clatter. A patient, vacant, blink
of cursor.

Seattle Woman Trying To Live On Sunlight Alone Is Probably Going To Die.

Freed
from the tyranny of kitchens, you have more time
        to notice things:

your hair and fingernails growing;
        the pranic power of breathing.

The hunger doesn't trouble you much

        after the first week or two.

                        You start to feel
a hollowing out, a kind of clarity.

                        Your dreams float
like sailboats on a tide of breath;

        they will fascinate you out of speaking.

The world spins slower now. Under my skin
        I can divine

                the first molecules of chlorophyll

sungazing me green and golden.

I am no longer

attached to these sensations, I have achieved

a full measure of remoteness. Ready to light-merge

I am an angel in training.

Is there

no sunlight here on fallback earth? Carry me outside.

I thought it would feel warmer.

Kim Göransson

Dear Conundrum

Modern Theologians

Dear Conundrum

There are flesh eating bacteria and they will surely kill me.
And that will be a kind of justice.
There are too many diseases and a large hole in my right sneaker.
Happiness is a kind of dying.
There are sun spots we can't see and certain elevations
where breathing becomes labored:
Your mouth is a failed rectangle.
Your mouth is glazed with surrender.
Certain angles. I am geometrically challenged.
Come a little closer. Behold the spectacle
of one's daughter cutting up fashion magazines
and applying too much glue.
We are the too much glue.
Last month's bodies hung out to dry.
These quiet alphabets
under the skin.
Bacteria has no shame: We are someone's bacteria.
Someone's shame is us: My hunchback deepens
with the slightest shift in the weather.
And surely the I is an experiment in masochism.
This void with a view.
A girl without hands sits on a horse and smiles.
America.
The jig is up.
The apocalypse was a rerun and a workshop.
To believe again.
Each prepackaged perfect realism.
We come with puppies deserving homes and free coat-hangers
with each purchase.
Bring your own shovel.

And all the eyes are post-production. Too much glue:
I love you.
It says on the teleprompter. Like you mean it. With big bold
letters.
Bye bye blackbird. I go to the library but
the library is crawling with cockroaches.
Shiny absences.
These are the telephones of tomorrow ringing.
Small fuckers over the arm. Poetry? A bald man
leaning in the biography section
creating an optical illusion.
A minor terrorist explosion.
Young people petting between the shelves.
Is the brain of a person the root or the fruit?
How much paint ends up inside a painter
who has painted all his life?
Through the skin, ingested, inhaled?
Mixed to a total grey.
Apologies?
Or wood the cellist. Lungs like tough ceramic
draped across the room.
Dear Conundrum.
Dear silence police.
Dear angry widows.
We are like flowers in a way, little damp hollows
that lead to nowhere

Modern Theologians

Now my daughter insists
Jesus did walk on water
and I got nothing
but how long should it really take
for an orchid to die without water?

So let the kids play their video games
as night falls.
It's true,
we are all capable of great acts of violence.

Laura Lee

Chorus

Chorus

All March it rained
or misted, cold splashes
my lungs full, yet I dreamt
on my sick bed
spring dreams, for I hoped–
with spring you would return.

Forsythia bloomed already.
Small furry buds on the lilacs,
yet you are still gone.
Today, walking near the swamp,
sneaking away from sickness
I heard them–the chorus frogs–
not full bodied singing just yet
too early for that, but they've returned
weeks early, all that rain and mist–
yet you are still gone.

Lee Webber

Eulogy

Eulogy

Mum said if I'd loved you I'd have seen you before the end,
but it was love that kept me away.
Your three month death-bed on the sterile palm of a ward,
spin-dried life lain out to dry.
Mum acted like she never saw it coming,
like you hadn't been gone for years. The day we took you to the
home,
the three of us sat on your unmade bed,
floating among your past. Your memories were now only things,
your footsteps a map of tea-stained tea-towels,
photographs and mugs. It was as though you knew you'd come to
forget,
and kept something back to remind you of you.
I don't feel like crying, I feel like punching a wall, ashamed at
what I can't mend,
at how we'd kept you there so long.
You never howled in pain or reproach, a prisoner numb to his
prison,
each new morning another crack in the paint
on a ceiling you couldn't quite see. That's why I couldn't go
before you died,
because I'd already seen the end.
I prefer to think of how you really were, the silence of your
shaking laughter,
how I was always the one to blame,
the way you'd turn everything off at the mains, even your sexist
jokes.
That was you and that's what I'll keep,
wishing I could promise that I won't forget, knowing that I might.
That was us – where we overlapped.

Lynn Blackadder

Tide

Tide

The yoghurt pot bobs like his penis (already warm) in the greying
plastic bath.
Sweat beads over large pores and drips down dirty blond strands
into a gannet stare.

The foil comes off, and he works at the cream with a cheap dull
spoon, each shovel clunking enamel. My fillings yelp.

The discarded vessel-utensil licks the maidenhair on the ledge he
uses to stand up.
From my seat I ask, 'Lived on your own long then?'

Lynsey Rose

Sundry

Extol

Sundry

The walls miss you.
The bed calls your name.
The bricks hold their breath.
They wait.
The sheets weep.
Your clothes pine, abandoned.
The food in the fridge counts the days
since you last opened their door.
The milk tells the mould that never knew you
stories of who you were.
Books lie paused,
Dishes delayed,
Blinds down.
The soft toys huddle in corners,
asking after you –
Which one saw you last?

Extol

I was wrong
before
about falling in
love being about
me.
And fitting together
is one thing
but I've never 'not'
fitted
with a lover.
All people fit
if you hammer hard
enough.
So love isn't that,
either.
Our love is about
light up deities,
pop gods
and seasides.
And how you came
from space to save
me,
did you know that?
The story is
upside down
from the way you
tell it.

Mikey Delgado

Rosh Hashana and The Railway Network of Europe, 1942.

Visiting Dean.

Before the rain comes the bees are reluctant to leave

Rosh Hashana and The Railway Network of Europe, 1942.

"…across all the beautiful landscapes of Europe…"

If with honeyed lips in this bitter place
I kiss your sweetened mouth,
through the slats of the cold, windowless wagon
we may spy apples on orchard trees.

And should there be none, in the cold starred night,
we shall still see them…rosy, ready to drop
into rough aprons; and we will turn to each other
and we will say "A sweet year my love." And
we will hear the other say "A sweet year my love."
And we will lie down, and we may never rise again.

Strange to think there could have been Spring
and Summer then, or even that some days were warm
with sunshine, and lovers would have casually
ambled under the limes.
And the blood-red sky at dusk…that it marbled blue heaven
with pink, promising beauty for the day to come
as ashes cool and we are nothing.
And we are nothing.

And that traincrews the entire length of Europe
rose from early warm beds, consulted roster boards,
rolled cigarettes of loose-leaf tobacco, and
marshalled wagons of the Jew-trains;
and station shunters wrote poems in their heads
while they switched boxcars
from Drancy and Westerbork and Theresienstadt,

daydreaming all the while of flaxen-haired Margarete
disrobed, reclining, readied.

And from the Low Countries to the territories
of the Pale of Settlement were maps
thick with black snakes
of the railway network of Europe, and,
mein Gott!…students of such matters enthuse…
it is muscular, visionary, efficient,
prioritised…troop trains, munitions, Jew trains,
timetabled to the cooling of ovens.

To imagine that then the grass
could have still grown green,
and that blossom-decked trees
in pink and white
could have decorated Europe
beside the clack of passing trains;
and to imagine that over the clack
of passing trains
people spoke grace over meals
as night came down…
and with their broken bread
mopped the last of delicious soup,
and their purple wine wet their thirsty mouths,
and, satiated, plans for the lifetimes
of children are made,
and the harvest…the harvest is fine,
and next year at least is assured.

Alpine rosemary and edelweiss
thrive far above the childish train snaking East;
and calls across the valley
from hillside to hillside
never mention war; and children

skip to schoolrooms and learn ideas,
and paint pictures in warm colours,
and the cleverest, wisest, smartest,
best-read child introduces *"dirty jew"*
and the *Knock on the Door* game
into the play; and at dawn
the ashes are raked.

And to imagine in the early twilight,
to glide under that arch to barking dogs
and knifing yellow light,
and even then to glance again back
to the direction from which you came,
and to see your God has dashed the sky red
with promise for a dry tomorrow...
and to know there will be no rain
to damp your ash.

Visiting Dean.

By the road to the mental hospital
a guy on the wall calls across to us
that he's starring in a Chinese movie
about the exploits of a gang of bandits.
He says he's reading a book called *Knots*.

Mindful of the long corridor
we still have to walk to the secure ward
I call back that *life's a scream*
and he opens his shirt to show to the sun
the tattoos he'd done when he'd come undone.

Haha, he howls, *life's a scream.*
That's true that is mate. I'll put that here.
And he draws a circle with his fingers
around where he thinks his heart should be,
next to the blue inked words *Man is born free.*

The long corridor is quiet. The floor
somehow sucks up the sounds of our shoes
and everyone we pass looks beatific.
On the other side of the secure door
they look at us like rabbits might look at war.

Dean is mellow. *Never tell them what you know,*
he whispers, as we pass into the garden.
He stretches on the grass and we take the bench.
Everything has form and content, he says.
When we go wrong the form contains the mess.

And the blue mottled clouds that hold rain
which once fell on Rutherford, New Jersey,
start to wash over us. *Clean my sins away,*
begs Dean, holding his arms open wide.
We smiled for him in there. When we left we cried.

Before the rain comes the bees are reluctant to leave

Before the rain comes the bees are reluctant
to leave their beloved purple.
Everywhere Master William's rough beasts
lumber along roads we've barely imagined,
slouching in their armed millions
towards all their Bethlehems. But really, who cares?
Not me. Not this afternoon. I'm safe. The barbaric wars
are far from here. *'A car is alkaline?'* Dear Caroline
has misheard me, shielding the lips I long to kiss
here by the pond where dragonflies flit over lilies,
where water-boatmen skip across the green shallow water.
We are hearing the sad language devalued, murmurs
some passer-by. Propaganda for war rises on the thermals
of a lunatic's breath and from the pergola we see other lovers
flitting between trees, fluttering about each other
with tiny fluctuations, like bees settling onto blossom.

By the *castanea sativa* I picture a kiss from Caroline's lips
melting glass, not to liquefied shards but to sugar water,
some sweet syrup into which even the early wasps
would be ardent to sink. The plump bees incite a leaning
towards her honey belly but in the belvedere in the warm wind
in late June bystanders mention those impostors of ours
who manoeuvre words *(reach out, shoulder to shoulder –*
even *Christian* if I cared anything about it) and somehow
the spell is broken and we turn instead towards the café,
and the conversation between us becomes only sensible.

The weather turns gloomy and the lightened lilac petals
on the south side of the ceanothus are changed to a darker blue

under the gathering clouds. The far-from-home waitress
becomes sullen in the early dusk. Above the café's muzak a voice
pretends to know the war is going well,
and the bees begin to leave their beloved purple
as the rain begins to patter against the terraced vines
and the miniscule insect fiefdoms there.

Nuala Ní Chonchúir

The Red Massey Ferguson

Elegy for a Flat

In Vitebsk there Lives a Cow

The Red Massey Ferguson

He styles her Blessed, Beloved,
straddles her to feel her exquisite torque;
when she won't turn over he wheedles
in tones a spinster might use on a cat:
'Whisha, come on, girl, be good now.'

She thrums to life and he pets her flank,
sits like a lord on her buckeye seat
and savours her judder beneath him.
After spinning up the boreen to the field,
they furrow, penetrate the earth's cushion.

On Sundays, they waltz out together to Mass,
a scarlet woman and her biddable man.

Elegy for a Flat

I fought, those mornings, with the zinc of the sky,
fought to push it back under the edge of the world,
to reclaim navy, star-pricked and moon-glowed.

The view of Blessington Street below us was
both wonder and curse; city sirens wheened,
we and the traffic beat our own rhythms.

I would soon wind down the stairs to the street,
take a last glance at the Basin and its island willow,
the redbricks opposite, rag-curtained and sad.

The road west stretched long ahead and I left,
hauling your flat with me, its air, its contours, you.
Still the east pulled on me like tide. It pulls still.

In Vitebsk there Lives a Cow

whose rolling eye is as loving as a mother's.
I go to her stall to breathe straw and dung,
to place cornmeal bread and potato scraps
between her lips, feel her spit drip onto my palms.

I place my cheek on her flank, warm with grass,
and hear her four stomachs pluck a tune;
this is her song to me – a Vitebsk lullaby.

At the *shtibel* I give thanks, '*Hallelujah*,' I cry
to a room small as prayer, and all heads turn.
Across the village, in her stall, my cow lows in reply,
while Мама pulls on her teats and *hiss* goes the bucket.

(After *I and the Village* – Marc Chagall)

Raewyn Alexander

past conversations rained on the roof

a complicated friend

past conversations rained on the roof

       tea may not mend days but it cures a few moments

inside a wooden box once made in class
the initials of his first girlfriend and a heart he carved

       they decided to accept answers with hoopla in them

life for some moments a fairground in the rain
after-hours with garish paint unlit

       empty of audience - whap whap tents and wind pecks

caravan window music moth feathery
dim mirror mazes and forgotten card tricks

       words form so they click open and build

while fear sat with her like someone else's dog
kindness generated better bedfellows and books

       a feline stalking the moon beyond water

a complicated friend

with touch-coded suitcase words
a (white) tulle dress in the rain
broken plastic gun near on the lawn
held breath
disappearing acts
extraordinarilyfastorcrowdedmomentswhereconfusionlives
and pays him rent
in cash

he's seated or running or getting up or down or on a walk
one hand holds a gadget
the other in his pocket warm as a bunny
softness makes him think of summer afternoons
but he rarely admits that except with blooded stories
 and crushes the page with loss on it
tosses the paper into flames which follow him everywhere

there at her shoulder even when he's away
or he's asleep and not to be awakened before
this number
dreams as private as his tattoo genesis
a lone dance where the clock of his mind fixes itself
stretched across a gravel path
video of a shadow
refuses to be filmed
mutates into an animal building a dam
chasing an idea until it turns into sticks

they watch each other closely like enemies
their laughter as disarming as sex

Richard Peabody

Yuletide Blues

Shoe Tree

Life After College

President Garfield Has Been Shot

Temple Garments

Yuletide Blues

A group of Freshmen sitting at a table
shooting the bull about the impending holidays.

Lots of privileged "I'm going to do this
or that, and go here or there."
Hang out with the buds from school.
Go skiing. Go to the movies. Fly to Aspen,
or LA, or Boulder, or Pasadena.
Eat goose. Eat turkey. Eat venison.
and lots and lots of pie—pecan,
pumpkin, and mince-meat.

Damn this is going to be the absolute best.
One guy silent. "What are you gonna do
over the holidays?" And then so quiet
nobody says a thing—"I'm going to
work in the mines."

Shoe Tree

(St. Mary's City, MD)

Nobody knows how many pairs of shoes
actually hang from the tree.
Impossible to get a precise count.

A pair of shoes hanging from a power line
frequently identifies a drug dealer's corner.

A pair of shoes hanging from a power line
just as frequently is nothing more than a prank.

But a tree filled with shoes? —tennis shoes,
hiking boots, running shoes, Topsiders,
you name it—that's symbolic of something fresh.

And here at the college it means just one thing—
somebody's done lost their virginity.

When you walk up under the shoe tree in the dark
and shine your flashlight into the branches
it seems to stir and vibrate with the
afterglow of a thousand orgasms.

And yet it's just a tree like any other.
Slick with rain today. Leaves beginning
to green and hide the shoes which appear
to be waiting for their wings to dry
so that they may lift off once the rain ebbs
and fly some place new and miles from here.

Life After College

So I worked at W. Bell in Rockville
during the day, in a warehouse
where Dread Zeppelin played in rotation
and worked at the Act IV bar in upper
Georgetown at night.

At the warehouse I used pneumatic tubes
to woo the sales girls in Catalog—we could
see each other through the glass—and I
whooshed poems and unattributed song lyrics
I remembered across to them.

I'd get smiles and laughter and a few
"Shouldn't you be working" notes in return.
No idea where the bravado came from.
One of the women at W. Bell was a friend
of my sister's. I didn't know any of the guys.

At night I lugged buckets of ice back and forth
from the Act IV to The Grog and Tankard—
My boss owned them both, as well as Babe's
and Simon's Pub. People drank and danced.
I washed dishes, supplied cherries, and ice
for the bar, policed drinks, and shared tips
with the bar staff and waitresses.

I was shy and didn't dance but made friends
with two bands—Tahoka and Facedancer.
They were a cut above any bar bands
particularly in 1973 as music was shifting
into disco.

Sleek women came to drink and dance and
one named TJ made it clear that she liked me.
So out of my league. Another gal got drunk
and wrapped her arms and long red hair
around me. Not something that had ever
happened in my virginal life.

The bartender said she was a stripper
at Good Guys down the block. No way.
"Oh yeah, if I were you I'd take her on home."
But he wasn't me. And as beautiful as she was—
such skinny little hips—I was way too chicken
to do anything about it.

And my life would go on like this—
burning the candle at both ends
until two things happened—

A young kid with the fuzzy Flo and Eddie afro
drove a delivery truck under W. Bell's overhang,
ripping off the metal roof and sending it airborne
almost hitting the store manager with the
flying debris.

And Halloween night at the bar
I was cleaning up by myself—like I always did—
when I found an enormous pile of puke
in the women's bathroom.

So there I was on my knees mopping up
the sickening smelly insides of some
kitty cat or cute vampire from hell—
and I had to use a brush and really
put some elbow grease into cleaning
the grout between the tiles

and it was taking forever

and I realized there had to be more to life
than this, more than driving home with
blue balls every night, more than being
so close to all of these woman who
might as well have been mannequins
in a store window.

President Garfield Has Been Shot

So his doctors give him "nutritional enemas"
of eggs, beef bullion, and whiskey.

Modern medicine's finest hour.

Medieval alchemists
in Ken Russell's *The Devils*,
attach jars filled with wasps and hornets
to the bodies of writhing patients.

My guess is that getting repeatedly stung
will take your mind off your sinus infection.

Garfield's doctors no better,
in prime Keystone Cops mode—
poke and prod the wound with their fingers,
fail to sterilize any instruments,
and operate without anesthesia.

Infection continues to spread.

Alexander Graham Bell tries
a metal detector-like device
to locate the bullet.

When this fails the doctors
attack the wound like guests
with bowls of silky Yule pudding
in search of the almond.

They compare hands to find
the longest digits, which they
jam into the wound.
One feels Garfield's liver.
Another finds a broken rib.

They rummage unwashed hands
around in Garfield's ravaged flesh
like messy toddlers eating Zwieback.

No surprise that Garfield dies soon after—
the bullet safely tucked in scar tissue
and no mortal danger at all.

Temple Garments

I knew that Mormons
didn't have horns or tails
but heard they wore wildly
creative zodiac-inspired
festive underwear.

Golden suns and moons and star signs
sprinkled across dark blue cotton.
Entire constellations I would trace
with lazy fingers before making
sacred honey love by the fireplace.

I wanted the "Song of Solomon"
and wound up with Marie Osmond.

How disappointing. I didn't expect
Victoria's Secret and yet this temple garb—
only white and rough with four simple
marks? The Square, which isn't a square at all
but a backwards L. The Compasses, which are
a V. (Did Thomas Pynchon lift that from the
Masons or here?) And the dashes at the navel
and right knee? Every knee shall bow
yet I keep flashing on the Trilateral Commission.

Maybe I need to date a Zoroastrian or
Rosicrucian? Maybe they have
bigger badder holier underwear?
The temple garments I imagined
chaste as long johns
just infinitely more interesting.

Be my North Star.
Your pert breasts my compass and square.

Sean Brijbasi

i (ultimately) tabitha

i (ultimately) tabitha

Little birds are chirping, but not because I feed them.

Today is Friday.

My leg is picking itself up and

a disaster looms in the next sentence.

The volcano erupted and destroyed the village.

But the villagers were already dead.

"What's your name?"

I have a plantigrade stroll and a winning smile. Not to mention

I think I'm turning my head sideways.

dot

People want this:

I had a good view of the café across the street where I would go
and sit when it wasn't busy. I could see somebody at my table and
I always wondered about the people who sat at my table. It was
easier than wondering about everybody. Today there was a young
woman writing a letter. Not many people write letters anymore I
thought and she seemed happy to be writing the letter. I almost
smiled but the tanks came through and blocked my view.

And I give them this:

History is peeing in my bed.

dot dot

People don't float, but people are floating. People should understand this.

Little birds are chirping because of electricity and not because I thumbed through my dictionary of coincidences.

A: Andalusian kiss.

I kissed a girl on her neck (who happened to be from Andalusia).

P: Periwinkle.

I spoke to a girl who had periwinkle eyes. The color of my bedroom slippers.

Which reminds me, I once met a girl and took her home, but she wouldn't take off her clothes. Later, I found out it was because her family was poor and her underwear had holes in it.

This will not be in the history books.

Today is not Friday.

Good things will or will not happen.

Monsters are lonely in dark, empty rooms.

Stephen Moran

In the Waiting Room of the Western Eye Hospital

In the Waiting Room of the Western Eye Hospital

I'm writing on my phone to while away
The crowded hours spent in this A and E.
A blur obscures my window, while the day
Unspools on Marylebone's evening street.
Here while taxis' amber lights go by,
A boy is screaming in the triage room.
The all-night clinic of the Western Eye
Hospital, where no one can see the gloom.
All are cheerful. Maisie, Mansoor, Abdul,
Concepta, Fatima. One or two have been
Here before and know the drill. They're full
Of London gallows humour often seen
When the worst comes to the best. But joy,
It's home for the fearful, now quiet boy.

Susan Campbell

I Never Think Of You

Sillage

I Never Think Of You

i was not thinking of you
when we set the lantern free

its huge yellow glowy globe
filled with fire

trailed behind the others
almost as if it would like to stay

confirmation that it had grasped each word
whispered as the four corners licked the match

and the red lantern that refused to rise
caught my dress and then rose on the gasps

frightened onlookers, girly girls in panic
somehow i'd catch alight and rise toward the tree

the yachts sent signals across the Tay
bobbing bobbins bidding bye bye

i did not think of you as you caught my hand
your eyes flashing warnings i ignored

red and yellow lanterns and yachts and twilight
still.

i did not think of you.

Sillage

The geese flew noisy en masse this morning
leaving for who knows where
I've no idea how long their journey
it seems they know the way instinctively

I wonder where your journeys led
and how you knew the way
if you stop off anywhere for coffee and a fag
the cigarette trails of strangers curl
towards me then disappear on an almost touch

I imagine it's you sending me secret whispers of move yourself
words like smile, laugh, breathe
keep moving. Keep moving.
nicotine caffeine fuelled love

sillage

Tim Craven

Smoking with a girl

Smoking with a girl

Just outside the backdoor of the bar,
overlooking the cramped parking lot,
we smoked cigarettes, leaving the others
to play pool. The gibbous moon, I said,
would shrink each night to nothing.
I paused to take a drag, the silence
broken by the crackle of the orange
ember advancing down the cigarette.
My smoking habit had doubled
since we'd met but this was when
I got her alone.

Vanessa Gebbie

The Bet

The bet

Before he died (The Man who Loved the Horses)
they called the priest to come round quick and pray.
The priest arrived on his bike
with the oil in a bag on his back.
He hadn't even shaved.

And when the priest had done,
The Man who Loved the Horses sat up and asked
for a biro, then passed his last hour
with The Racing Post, ringing
the winners in the next meeting
at Sligo.

Contributors

Raewyn Alexander lives in New Zealand and buys trees for travel when she globe-trots. She writes novels, stories, poetry, non-fiction and lectures Narrative Writing at UNITEC. Her blog is read world-wide and she's had fifteen books published along with many poems, stories and other work. At Happy Tea House she presents various literary events and has done for nine years. More here: http://poeticjourneytoamerica.blogspot.co.nz/

Alex Barr's poetry collections are *Henry's Bridge* (Starborn 2008) and *Letting In The Carnival* (Peterloo 1984.) He won third prize in the National Poetry Competition 2000. At present he is working mainly on short stories. His most recent poetry work is a collaboration with Peter Oram of Starborn Books on *Orchards,* a verse translation of Rilke's French collection *Vergers.* He taught architecture at Manchester Metropolitan University but now lives on a smallholding in West Wales with his wife Rosemarie, a ceramic artist.

Lynn Blackadder lives in Kilburn, London, where she writes poetry and fiction and attends Willesden Green Writers' Group. Her work has been shortlisted by the Bridport Prize and Liars' League. Lynn also coaches arts and heritage leaders and in her spare time pursues a lifelong interest in moral philosophy.

Sean Brijbasi lives in America. Sometimes he writes.

James Browning Kepple is the founder of Underground Books.org. He is the current judge of the annual New York City High School wide Poetry Competition sponsored by the New York Browning Society. His 6th collection of Poetry, "Thus Virginia Passes" is available now with Pretend Genius Press. He enjoys long walks on the beach, the scent of your hair etc, etc...

Susan Campbell is an unfinished poem. She can be found bobbing and weaving through the days of her life like a tapestry needle full of neon thread in Dundee, Scotland.

David Cooke won a Gregory Award in 1977 and published his first collection, Brueghel's Dancers in 1984. His retrospective collection, In the Distance, was published in 2011 by Night Publishing and a collection of more recent pieces, Work Horses, has recently been published by Ward Wood Publishing. His poems, translations and reviews have appeared widely in journals including Agenda, Ambit, The Bow Wow Shop, The Critical Quarterly, The Irish Press, The London Magazine, Magma, The North, Orbis, Other Poetry, Poetry Ireland Review, Poetry London, Poetry Salzburg Review, The Reader, The SHOp and Stand.

Tim Craven. Originally from Stoke-on-Trent, Tim recently moved from North-West London to New York having been accepted onto Syracuse University's creative writing MFA program. His poems have appeared in Anon, Fourteen, The Interpreter's House, Obsessed with Pipework and Envoi.

Mikey Delgado still hasn't served in the navy or attended university or been drawn to Germanic folklore. He is the author of the novel "Life and War with Mikey Fatboy Delgado" (Laughing Mushroom Press, 2010) and the forthcoming novel "Geology of the Railroad Earth" (Laughing Mushroom Press – due March 5th 2014). http://laughingmushroompress.blogspot.com/

Vanessa Gebbie is Welsh but lives in the south of England with her family. She writes short stories, poems, and novels. She is author of two collections of short fiction, one poetry pamphlet and one and a half novels. She is also contributing editor of Short Circuit, Guide to the Art of the Short Story, editions 1 and 2. www.vanessagebbie.com

Kim Göransson is a native of Sweden but resides in the higher bible belt of rural America. He has a family. He sometimes writes poetry and fronts the one-man band My Hot Air Balloon.

Charles Lambert was born in 1953 in England but, apart from brief spells in Ireland, Portugal and London, has lived and worked in Italy since 1976. He is the author of two novels, Little Monsters and Any Human Face, a novella, The Slave House, and a collection of prize-winning stories, The Scent of Cinnamon and Other Stories. His new novel, The View from the Tower, and a work of autobiographical fiction, With A Zero at its Heart, will be published in 2014.

Laura Lee is a teacher and writer from the United States. She has been published in journals from Chicago to New Zealand.

Andrew Mayne was born and raised in South Africa, in a province called Transvaal that no longer exists. But this was, overall, probably a good thing because it meant the end of Apartheid. He moved to London, fell in with the Willesden Green Writers' Workshop which met in the Willesden Green library. This library no longer exists either. It's difficult to see how this could ever be a good thing. He moved to Ireland in 2005 towards the end of the Celtic Tiger. The Celtic Tiger also no longer exists.

Geraldine Mills has published two collections of short stories and four collections of poetry. She has been awarded many prizes and bursaries including the Hennessy/Tribune New Irish Writer Award, an Arts Council Bursary and a Patrick and Katherine Kavanagh Fellowship. Her fiction and poetry are taught in universities in Connecticut, U.S.A. Her third short story collection titled Hellkite is forthcoming from Arlen House.

Stephen Moran is a writer and editor based in London. He has published a collection of short stories, The London Silence (Pretend Genius, 2004), and a small number of stories and poems in anthologies and magazines. He is married with one grown-up son and a day job. Website: www.stephenmoran.net

Nuala Ní Chonchúir was born in Dublin in 1970; she lives in East Galway. Her fourth short story collection *Mother America* was published by New Island in 2012; *The Irish Times* said of it: 'Ní Chonchúir's precisely made but deliciously sensual stories mark her as a carrier of Edna O'Brien's flame.' Her début novel *You* (New Island, 2010) was called 'a gem' by *The Irish Examiner* and 'a heart-warmer' by *The Irish Times*. A chapbook of short-short stories is forthcoming in the US in September.

Richard Peabody is a French toast addict and native Washingtonian. He has two recent books out–a book of poetry Speed Enforced by Aircraft (Broadkill River Press), and a book of short stories Blue Suburban Skies (Main Street Rag Press). He won the Beyond the Margins "Above & Beyond Award" for 2013. He has edited Gargoyle Magazine since back before Elvis died.

Lynsey Rose studied BA Writing and Publishing at Middlesex University and now works for a charity as a magazine and web editor. Her first novel First Aid Kit Girl, a black comedy about a self-harming office worker, was published earlier this year by The Green Press to rave reviews, and is available on Amazon. Lynsey writes the blog, 'Exitainment' in which she rants enthusiastically about TV, music, books, feminism and film. Read it at lightupvirginmary.blogspot.co.uk.

Judi Sutherland is a survivor of corporate life and a graduate of the Creative Writing MA at Royal Holloway. Her work has been published in The Interpreter's House, Oxford Poetry, Acumen, Ink, Sweat & Tears, and other places. She's working towards that important first collection and writing her first novel. Her blog is at www.judisutherland.com.

Lee Webber is 30 years old and has been living in London for the past 6 years. His poetry has been shortlisted for the Bridport Prize and appeared in a 'Hidden Talent' issue of the online publication Beat the Dust. He works for University College London coordinating clinical trials in cancer research.

Also in this series from Pretend Genius Press

last night's dream corrected

Raewyn Alexander, Richard Atkinson, Bill Berkson,
J. Tyler Blue, Sean Brijbasi, Terri Carrion, Ira Cohen,
Josh Davis, Mikey Delgado, Stratos Fountoulis,
Kim Göransson, Susan Kennedy, Joanne Kyger,
Elias Miller, Stephen Moran, Michael Rothenberg,
Dean Strom, Blem Vide, Richard Wright

isbn: 0-9747261-6-8

www.ingramcontent.com/pod-product-compliance
Lightning Source LLC
Chambersburg PA
CBHW051731040426
42447CB00008B/1077